Sacrament, Wholeness and Evangelism

A Catholic Approach

Stephen Cottrell

Missioner with *Springboard*
the Archbishop of Canterbury and York's Initiative in Evangelism

GROVE BOOKS LIMITED
RIDLEY HALL RD CAMBRIDGE CB3 9HU

Contents

'I have come that you may have life and have it in abundance'
(John 10.10)

The questions at the end of each chapter could be used in discussion groups
or by a PCC to pick up on specific aspects of this booklet.

The Cover Illustration is by Peter Ashton

First Impression February 1996
Reprinted February 1999
ISSN 0953-4946
ISBN 1 85174 309 X

1

Being Before Doing:
A Model for the Missionary Church

On my first Sunday as a parish priest there were about sixty people in church for the Parish Communion at 9.30 am. My wife was the youngest person there, I was the second youngest. The service was dignified and predictable—not so much dull as lacking in energy and expectation. It was all over in an hour. A dozen people stayed for a pretty horrible cup of coffee and by eleven o'clock I was back in the vicarage wondering what to do for the rest of the week. Nothing in my expensive training for ministry had prepared me for this moment. I was a vicar (well, actually, a priest-in-charge), but the job that was needed was a missionary. In that moment I experienced what I now describe as a call within a call. I realized God wanted me to be a mission priest. Because I became a Christian within the catholic wing of the Church of England all I did in that parish to proclaim and promote the Christian faith and to help the church to grow arose out of my catholic spirituality. I offer it to Christians of all traditions because it worked, and because I believe the catholic approach to evangelism has much to offer contemporary culture.

Most of this booklet is theoretical, but at the end of each chapter I have briefly reflected how these ideas worked themselves out in the reality of a growing church.

I am now the Missioner in the Wakefield diocese and am involved in encouraging and equipping churches for mission. I still return to the basic ideas outlined here as the best way of discovering what it means to be a missionary church. I also work as an evangelist. Although this is about being an evangelistic church, I do believe in challenging to make a decision for Christ; commitment is still the vital step of faith. What experience has shown me is that in a culture far distanced from the Christian tradition there are many second miles to travel before that point of decision arrives. But that is jumping the gun.

My first step in trying to revitalize the church was to present a vision of what I felt God was calling us to be. Out of this we would discover what he wanted us to do. This was the principle upon which renewal and mission were based; what we do as a church ought to arise out of what we are called to be.

In the Nicene Creed the church is called *'holy, catholic and apostolic.'* Holy means *being in communion with God.* Catholic means *being in community with one another.* Apostolic means *being in communication with the world.*

This is what the church is called to *be.* If what we *do* arises out of this then the church has only three priorities—*Worship, Nurture* and *Outreach.*

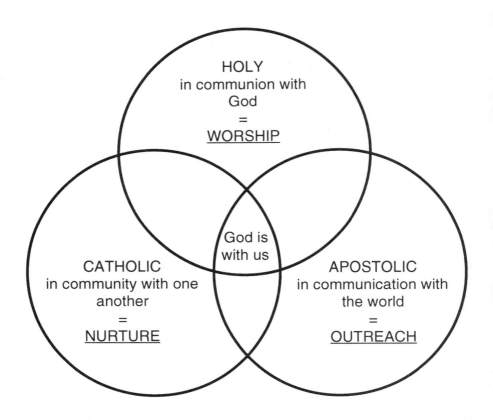

Figure 1: A Model for the Missionary Church

Together these three form the mission of the church for they encompass its primary *call*—to worship God and be in relationship with him—and its primary *commission*—to make disciples (Matthew 28.19). Making disciples involves outreach *and* nurture. We are to share with others the fullness of life we have received from Christ.

The overlaps also indicate how these different areas of the church's life are not compartments. Each area flows from and into another. Our life in Christ finds its destination in worship—in actual church services, in a personal life of prayer and, ultimately, with God in heaven. This worship is sustained by outreach and nurture.

I am indebted to John Cole, Diocesan Missioner for the Lincoln diocese, for this model of church which I have only slightly adapted from his excellent, and now sadly out of print, *How to be a Local Church*. Robert Warren has a similar diagram in his book *Building Missionary Congregations*. He makes the point that at the intersection of the three circles lies the energy for the mission of the church which is spirituality. This is what shapes and informs everything else.

I shall begin with a discussion about catholic spirituality, which must be the starting point. I will then look at the importance of the church as the agent of mission, then at the catholic approach to outreach, dealing specifically with the circle of outreach and the two overlaps with worship and nurture. In particular I will look at service to the community, the evangelistic power of the sacraments, the detailed relationship between nurture and evangelism and the pursuit and attraction of holiness.

Sometimes catholic Christians feel ill equipped for mission. I hope this booklet will provide inspiring theology and practical encouragement.

The church does not *have* missions, the church *is* a mission. Although this booklet is about evangelism, it is much more about being an evangelistic church. Worship, nurture and outreach are the triple focus of the church's mission and provide the framework for understanding catholic evangelism. Individual conversion must lead to corporate faith. However, many churches in the catholic tradition are not evangelistic. They have neglected the interplay of these three elements which make up their life. The challenge of evangelism, and hopefully of this booklet, is to restore harmony and balance between the different priorities of the church, and to see the creative potential of the overlap between the different areas.

For other churches I hope that a clearer understanding of catholic spirituality, and an enthusiastic introduction to catholic practice, will encourage exploration into the rich treasures of a common inheritance. One of the most exciting things that God is doing in our day is shuffling the pack of different traditions. The catholic understanding of church, worship, spirituality, sacrament and pilgrimage are vital for a healthy church.

All that is written here is reflection upon the actual experience of working to make a church grow. I dedicate it to the wonderful people of the parish where I served, especially the faithful sixty who were there on that first Sunday and who stuck with it as the church doubled in size.

Putting It Into Practice

As well as providing an illustration for the mission of the church, this model can also be a useful tool for developing a missionary strategy. As I tried to renew the vision for a church that was experiencing spiritual atrophy, considering our life under the three headings of worship, nurture and outreach proved invaluable. At an open meeting of the whole church this vision was agreed. We found that we were measuring our life against a commonly owned vision for what God wanted the church to be and not just the latest ideas of a new vicar.

To create a simple strategy for mission we asked ourselves these questions of each area:

- What is good and needs affirming and developing?
- What is not working and needs discarding or replacing?
- What is missing and needs introducing?

I now realize that this is a very basic mission audit. It is easy to do once the vision is agreed. It forms a natural and practical way of enfleshing the ideas of this booklet in ordinary communities of faith.

By working in this way we were quickly able to establish some gospel priorities and then create a plan for action. When tensions and disagreements arose, as they inevitably did, people found themselves wrestling with God, not with the vicar! The exciting journey of becoming a church for the world had begun.

Further Questions
- What does your church do? How does this reflect what the church is called to be?
- Have you ever prepared a mission statement for the church? Or a mission strategy?

2

Human Before Christian:
A Catholic Spirituality for Growth

At his birth Jesus is given two names. First, he is called *Jesus*, which means 'God saves'; 'he is the one who is to save his people from their sins' (Matthew 1.21). But, in fulfilment of the prophecy in Isaiah, he is also called *Emmanuel*, 'a name which means "God-is-with-us"' (Matthew 1.23).

At the heart of catholic evangelism is the belief that before you can really *know* Jesus as the God who saves, you have to *experience* him as the God who is with us. All Christians acknowledge this dynamic, but it is the particular emphasis of catholic theology and spirituality and shapes the distinctive contribution made to evangelism by catholic Christians. It is the starting point for this study and, having established the incarnational heart of catholic evangelism, what follows will show how this spirituality overflows into the catholic understanding of worship, nurture and outreach.

We begin with Emmanuel. The journey of faith begins with God's movement towards us. He is not a remote figure beckoning us from a distance, neither is he just a signpost pointing in the right direction—he is our companion on the road. Through his Spirit dwelling within us Jesus is like an inner homing device, adjusting to each wrong turn we make and leading us home. He has come to share our life on earth. The important point here is that he is our companion *before* he is our guide. He meets us on the path of our lives and walks with us.

This disclosure of love presents us with the great paradox of Christian faith. God is everywhere, but in order to know him we have to experience him somewhere. He is present and active in all situations, in all creation, in every time, every age and in every human heart, but to most people he is only dimly recognized, still less acknowledged. A good many people, a huge number in our own culture, do not recognize him at all, finding other ways to explain and understand the many signs around us of his loving presence. The *everywhere* God has to become the *somewhere* God. Therefore, at the heart of Christian faith is the Incarnation, God who is known as Emmanuel.

Identification and Proclamation

We worship a God who is sovereign lord of all creation, but who is emptied of what it means to be God in order to *know* what it is to be human. We have so sentimentalized Christmas that this paradoxical and radical message is easily lost. (Sometimes I wonder whether our round of carol services and nativity plays are anything more than a mass programme of inoculation—give people a little bit of the virus and they will be immune for the rest of their lives!) Where is God at Christmas? Why, he is screaming his head off in a makeshift cradle in an animal feeding trough at the back of a pub. He is having his nappy changed.

The first word of the gospel is Emmanuel. God is with us. He has come and visited his people. He has identified himself totally with our condition. In Jesus God has experienced human life from the inside. Before anything else Jesus is one of us.

This strong belief in the Incarnation is the root of catholic spirituality. From it flows the whole understanding of church and sacrament. From it also comes the *method* for evangelism.

Catholic evangelism begins with identification with those with whom the gospel is to be shared. In order for it to be shared it has to be incarnated both in the life of those who are trying to share it and in the community of those with whom it is being shared. The gospel message cannot be separated from a gospel community, a gospel lifestyle and a gospel service to the world. Bishop Michael Marshall loves to remind us, 'When the worship is over the service begins!'

The Magnificent 'Yes'

When God wanted to communicate his love to the world, he focused his everywhere in the somewhere of the womb of the Virgin Mary. He did not send a message of love, but a loving messenger. He also did this in such a way as to preserve our freedom of response. We will return to this theme later on, but suffice to say here, Mary could have said 'no.' But God's mission of salvation to the world began with her complete cooperation to his will: her magnificent 'yes.' So the catholic evangelist will try to make his or her whole life an incarnation of the gospel, will seek to cooperate with the will of God, will try to say 'yes.'

The extraordinary faithfulness of Mary to the word of God is a source of unending wonder to catholic Christianity, but is best understood in terms of evangelism. Mary is the first evangelist, because she is the one who bears God's word to the world. She enjoys God's favour (Luke 1.29). In her the word is enfleshed, grace has come into the world. St Augustine, speaking of Mary's faithfulness, said how she conceived Jesus in her heart *before* she conceived him in her womb. In other words she is living her whole life in openness to the will of God. This provides a model for mission. It begins with obedience to the word of God. It bears fruit in the formation of Jesus in the life of the believer. It is made possible by the gracious and creative brooding of the Holy Spirit. We become God-bearers in our flesh. We are filled with grace. 'All of us, with our unveiled faces, like mirrors reflecting the glory of the Lord, are being transformed into the image that we reflect in brighter and brighter glory; this is the working of the Lord who is Spirit' (2 Corinthians 3.18). Thus we know that the best form of evangelism is the Christ-like, Spirit-filled *example* of ordinary Christian people living the Christian life. The words of St Francis resonate in the heart of catholic Christianity: 'Preach the gospel to the whole world; use words if you have to.'

This is the reason we always find Jesus leading people into relationship with him, and through him to the Father. The message of the Christian faith is relationship with a messenger! This is the reason Jesus often refuses to answer many of the questions that are put to him, or else he turns them on their head, jabbing back with one of his disturbing and provocative stories. The message is relationship with God. We will discover he is the God who saves when we have first experienced him as the God who is with us. It has to be that way round. Otherwise we end up with a neat gospel separated from relationship. It is when this happens that Christianity can become judgmental and triumphalist: very cold and hard. The catholic witness to the Incarnation is vital to keep the whole of our evangelism Emmanuel-centred.

We are on a journey to wholeness—the word catholic means 'that which accords to wholeness'—and our faith is about the whole of life, not just about signing people up.

The Way to Ourselves

The Christian doctrine of humanity is that in Christ we can become ourselves. We can rediscover a potential that was lost. We can become what God has always intended us to be. Fullness of life is to be discovered both in right relationship with God, and also in right relationship with one another, with one's own self and with the whole of creation. As we discover the way to this wholeness we tread the way of holiness and Jesus is formed in us. We find him as not only the way to the Father, but the way to be ourselves. This is enormously attractive. It is in the bloodstream of catholic Christianity that holy lives and holy communities will draw people to them like flowers opening to the sunlight of a new day. Therefore so much of catholic evangelism remains unseen by those who, for equally good reasons, follow a more campaigning style. But the recent research of John Finney in *Finding Faith Today* and the writing of Robert Warren in *Building Missionary Congregations* and *Being Human, Being Church* point to the catholic emphasis of journey into faith and growing living communities of faith as points of reference for a full and wholesome Christianity. It is the unravelling of these two emphases in the form of a strategy for mission which will run through the rest of this booklet.

The aim of the Christian faith is to be fully human. So much evangelism has been the other way round, trying to turn human beings into Christians, often preaching a dislocated message without introducing people first to a loving messenger. Jesus wishes to turn Christians into full human beings! It is the same in the world. We try to turn children into adults, and Jesus wants to turn adults into children!

The heart of the gospel proclamation—the intersection of the three circles—must be Jesus the word made flesh, Emmanuel, amazing grace come upon the world. Faith is the way of life, a means to be fully alive with all the glorious potential that God has freely given us.

Putting It Into Practice

All churches have a spirituality, but it is often one of decline. Spirituality is about our self understanding of who we are in relationship to God. Some churches see themselves as a righteous remnant, a faithful few being buffeted and tossed about in a sea of relativism and unbelief, without hope that anything can ever be different. There is some truth in these images. The Bible often describes the people of God in similar ways. However, the church is not just the light in the darkness, but the light the darkness cannot overcome, the light which we are called to bear courageously into the darkness of the world, having no fear since Christ has already won the victory. Nothing else can change in a church until our self-understanding is renewed, and this has to be done before the mission audit exercise described at the end of the last chapter can really be of value.

In my experience this can only be done through prayer and through a bold envisioning of the church through word and example. I preached at every service about what it meant to be fully Christian, fully alive. I worked to establish a daily pattern of prayer in church, especially a daily Eucharist, and to foster, through prayer groups, house groups and times away together, a prayerful waiting on God and an expectation that he would energize us for mission and for life.

I know another church where the people chose to leave their building and go and worship in a hall because they felt an urgent need for a renewed vision of what it meant to be the people of God. At a key meeting the churchwarden spoke movingly of how the clergy had often taught them that God was the potter and they were the clay. 'Well,' he said, 'when a potter does not like what he has made he doesn't throw the clay away, but pushes it down and reshapes it into something new. That is what God is going to do with us.' They embarked upon an exodus of rediscovery and are now a growing church.

Further Questions

- How would you describe the spirituality of your church?
- What is your experience of finding God somewhere?

3
Belonging Before Believing:
The Corporate Nature of Faith

After his Ascension all Jesus leaves behind him is a group of people with whom he is in relationship. His instructions are very few. He has made it clear that he is the fulfilment of what we now know as Old Testament Scripture. He has told his followers that they must love one another with the same radical love that he has demonstrated. He has instituted a meal, a new Passover in remembrance of his death and resurrection, and he has taught them a prayer which articulates the heart of his teaching. But basically what you are left with is a small group of people.

It can be no coincidence that there is nothing else. No detailed regulations. No answers to the many theological problems that quickly arise. Nothing but a little community that had learnt, by being with Jesus, to live a new life of love. This community is called the church, and although its exterior life has changed massively over the years, it is still the same today. The church is essentially that group of people centred on Jesus and commissioned by him to live out, and share with others, this new way of living.

The story of the first Christian community as told in the Acts of the Apostles makes it clear that the dynamism of their love was enormously attractive, and many people joined this community because they saw within it a hope for their lives and for the world.

But we need to remember that at that time this church still had no clear doctrine, no recognized credal formulas, no scriptures apart from the Old Testament, no systematic theology. What they did have was the New Testament—not at this time a book, but a new relationship with God that had been created by Jesus, the new Adam, and therefore a new humanity. Out of this, as disputes and problems inevitably arose and as new challenges beckoned and as new experiences were absorbed, doctrine and Scripture and creed came to be formed, but at the heart was this Jesus-centred community.

The whole doctrine and theology of the Christian church is a reflection upon the experience of what God has done in Jesus Christ and upon the lived experience of the church as it sought to understand what this meant. *Now* we are able to say that these truths, enshrined in Scripture and in the traditions and creeds of the church, are true and unchanging for all time and all generations, but *then* it was a group of people loving one another and loving God and trying to make sense of the amazing things they had been witness to.

This simple understanding of the primacy of the church is very important to catholic Christianity. Although the highest regard is given to Scripture and to tradition and creed, it is always held within the context of the faith community. You cannot come to relationship with Jesus without coming to relationship with the church. Put simply, you cannot be a Christian by yourself. It is not a private option. Paul describes the church as a body with Christ at the head (or should we say the heart?). Just as you cannot be a member of a body on your own so you cannot be a Christian by yourself. It is the very nature of faith that it is communal and relational. In that community we are still being led into new truth and new ways of expressing the unchanging faith we have received. This faith is unchanging not because it is cast in stone, rigid and unbending, but because it is essentially relationship with a person, Jesus. His love is steadfast. He is unchanging in his faithfulness to us.

A Group Dynamic

There is one vital aspect I have left till last. In saying that all Jesus left behind him was a group of people, a group charged with precious responsibility to carry forward his mission of love to the world, it does not mean he abandoned that group. The greatest truth of the Christian faith is the exact opposite. Through the gift of the Holy Spirit Jesus is with his friends always, empowering them for ministry and mission, enabling them to become themselves and creating them as his church. The grace that was given to Mary, that was promised to all humanity (Joel 3.1), is now available through the Spirit. This is why we celebrate Pentecost as the birthday of the church.

This tremendous experience of the Holy Spirit was God's greatest gift of himself to the infant church. It was also, theologically, their first, and perhaps greatest, problem. How were they to make sense of the one God they all believed in, but who had also manifested himself to them as the Son Jesus, God and man, and now as Holy Spirit coming from Jesus and the Father? In the writings of the New Testament we find the foundational doctrine of Christianity, the understanding of God as Holy Trinity, beginning to emerge. God is within himself a community of persons—personal, relational and communal. The great miracle of love is that the infant church mirrors the nature of God, also a community of love. In every age the church is called to be the same community identified by the same marks of love.

If the evangelistic *message* of the gospel is about the fullness of life, the evangelistic *method* is relationship. This is the heart of Jesus' invitation: 'Come and see' says Jesus to Andrew (John 1.39); 'Follow me' to Peter (Mark 1.18). The most effective evangelism will often begin with the same invitation: come and experience a community of love. This will lead to an understanding of the beliefs which underpin that community's life. But it will be this way round. Catholic evangelism will be concerned with the creation of an evangelistic, missionary community. Prayer, worship and service to the wider community will all try to model an alternative lifestyle marked by a self-giving love that is not looking for any rewards save that God be praised in all that is done. As belief develops, and as important steps of commitment are made, it will constantly be nurtured by be-longing within the community. The emphasis will not be on 'my faith' or 'your faith' but *'our* faith.'

Putting It Into Practice

Churches need to model an alternative lifestyle of love and show service to the community (this is a theme developed in the next chapter). One of the ways this manifested itself in my experience was the setting up of a Parish Care Centre for the community. Here people could find a listening ear, a cup of coffee and practical, everyday help in a number of areas of life from filling in a tricky DHSS form to a listening ministry for the sad, the lonely or the bereaved.

Along with other similar initiatives, especially work with schools and young people, the life of the church as a fellowship of love was nurtured by prayer, but focused into the wider community. The fruits of this was the creation of a large fringe of people who were in contact with the church as an instrument of service.

Other churches have developed all sorts of ways of serving the community— parent and toddler groups, bereavement counselling, clubs for the elderly, men's groups and women's groups, social clubs—the list is endless. It begins with the understanding that the *raison d'être* of the church is the need of the world.

Further Questions

- If you were asked to draw a picture of your church, what would you draw?
- What words would you use to describe your church?

4

Listening Before Speaking:
Service at the Heart of Outreach

Service to the community is often the first mark of outreach. The spirituality and the message of the Christian faith are about fullness of life. The dynamic of this life is relationship. When we realize what God has called us to be, we can find what he wants us to do. The diagram in Chapter 1 specifically uses the word outreach not evangelism. Not only are worship, nurture and outreach all evangelistic, but evangelism is often best expressed by what we do, not by what we say. 'When you did it to the least of these my brothers and sisters,' says Jesus, 'you did it to me' (Matthew 25.40).

We see this approach in nearly everything that Jesus says and does. His first concern is to meet the needs of those he encounters. The gospel is not here a message or a messenger but an act of service and love. Jesus demonstrates this at the Last Supper when he washes the feet of his disciples and gives them the new commandment to love one another (John 13.34). They are able to do this because he has loved them. It is also demonstrated in the moving little episode in Luke's Gospel where a woman with a bad name, often thought to be Mary Magdalene, serves Jesus, washing his feet with her tears and drying them with her hair. Jesus notes that she is able to give much because she has received much (Luke 7.47). Here again is the overlap between worship and outreach. We receive from God and are therefore able to serve others. We do not do this for our own self-fulfilment (though it is extraordinarily fulfilling—in giving we receive) but in order to share the love we have received. We hope this will lead to relationship with God, but we do not do it for this reason. Love looks for no reward other than the giving of itself.

It is also interesting to note that, at the beginning of the episode where Mary Magdalene washed Jesus' feet, the Pharisees are moaning about Jesus. Their complaint is of great significance. Jesus ought to know what a bad woman she is (Luke 7.39). He is mixing with the wrong sort (see Luke 5.30). He meets these people on their own ground, shares their table and is prepared to listen and get to know them. Worse still, he shows love and service to them.

Jesus always has a ready ear for those with whom he comes into contact. He listens to the woman at the well (John 4.1-30), to the Syro-Phoenician woman (Mark 7.24-30), and most remarkable of all, when you consider it is the first Easter day, to Cleopas and his companion on the road to Emmaus (Luke 24.13-35). His first words are, 'What is it you are talking about as you walk along?' (Luke 24.17).

Jesus is concerned to build relationship. He is interested in people for who they are. He has a word for each person, but it is particular before it is universal.

It also involves dialogue. Alongside the requirement to make disciples, we must place the requirement to love our neighbour (Mark 12.31). The constant seeking after wholeness in evangelism which is at the heart of the catholic approach will mean that these two demands will be held in a creative tension and will often proceed by way of conversation before conversion. We begin with the desires and needs of those whom we meet. Before beginning on our agenda we listen to the needs of others. Then we are able not only to say a word that is relevant, but bring to fruition in Christ the good that is already within most people. This still requires a decision to follow Christ. In the end becoming a Christian is always an act of the will, something we decide to do, but it allows for real dialogue and exchange.

The supreme act of service in the life of Jesus is his death. A catholic understanding of the cross stems from the Incarnation. Just as God in Christ shares our birth, so also he shares our death. The cross is a sharing and complete identification with humanity. We also see it here as an example of self-giving love. I think it is for both these reasons that catholic Christians adore the presence of Christ on the cross as well as his victory over death symbolized by the empty cross. The cross, as well as expressing doctrinal truth about the nature of Christ's sacrificial death, also demonstrates his sharing of humanity and his service to humanity.

'I am with you always, even to the end of time,' says Jesus (Matthew 28.20). 'If you do it to the least of these my brothers and sisters you do it to me' (Matthew 25.40). These words lead catholic Christians to believe that the Incarnation is as much a present reality as the Crucifixion and Resurrection. Jesus is still with us. He can be encountered in the world. Therefore the focus of mission is the needs of the world, not the numerical advance of the church, and the method of mission will always be service. Because this understanding of mission is shaped by the Incarnation and sustained by an experience of God in worship there is a strong sacramental emphasis both in the worship and in the mission.

Sacramental Encounter

In worship the sacraments, especially the Eucharist, are points of encounter with a living Lord. In mission the same Lord is encountered in the world. And our response to Jesus, for it is him we minister to in others, is service. There is real adoration in evangelism.

The sacraments themselves are also evangelistic. Through the activity of the Holy Spirit they continue the ministry of Jesus. He is still present drawing people to the Father in baptism as he did throughout his ministry: feeding his people in the Eucharist as he fed the 5,000; healing his people in the sacrament of anointing as he healed blind Bartimaeus; forgiving his people in the sacrament of reconciliation as he forgave the woman caught in adultery. The word sacrament means a pledge. As he pledged to be with us for all time, so he is faithful to his promises. The sacraments provide an objective encounter with the risen Jesus, a sure channel of grace through which the Spirit is poured. They do not depend upon the eloquence or ability of the minister but only on God's faithfulness. In our own day sacramental worship and ministry can be particularly powerful. Sacraments point away from the personality of the minister. In an individualistic culture which exalts personality it is too easy for this to conceal the face of Christ. They also speak in a language our culture understands, involving all the senses and exciting the imagination. But they are still objective, the sacraments of the whole church. Through the word of the gospel, spoken by the priest with the authority of the church, through the physical sign of the sacrament itself and through the activity of the Spirit, Jesus is made present to his people. It is something tangible. It is not just that Jesus unites your life to his and gives you a share in the fruits of his sacrificial death and resurrection; there is actual water to be immersed in, to drown and rise in. It is not just that Jesus feeds you with his risen life; there is actual bread and wine to eat and drink. It is not just that Jesus heals you; there are hands laid on your head, there is oil on your forehead and on your hands. It is not just that Jesus forgives you; there is another human being, albeit a sinner like you, to announce to you personally Jesus' words of forgiveness and love.

These sacraments are powerful evangelism. They show the presence of Jesus in the church and for the world; they continue his ministry. They draw people to Christ and through Christ to the Father. They need to be expressed in such a way that allows the power of the sign to speak simply and tellingly. They need to be set free from some of the ecclesiastical clutter and cultural baggage that has weighed them down, but so released they remain Jesus' greatest gifts to his church. Through the sacraments Jesus serves his people. He is again the servant king whose glory is now veiled in water, bread and oil. As at the upper room to his first friends, so to us today; Jesus kneels before us and washes our feet.

Service, as the most vital expression of outreach, is about Christ's service to the world, and our meeting Christ in those we serve. It is about encounter and love. This will be expressed in the actual meeting of the needs of our community and this will begin with listening and finding out what is needed. It is about seeing where we can reach out with love to those around us. But it should also be powerfully sacramental, recognizing that the sacraments are there to minister Christ's grace to his people, to remind us of his presence in all those to whom we minister, and to lead us to a greater adoration of his presence in all creation.

Putting It Into Practice

I have thought through all the different people who became Christians in the church where I served to see what common links there might be. First, contact was established as service. Usually there was dialogue—a deliberate attempt to take seriously people's need to question and explore before a commitment could be made. Much of this was expressed through the process of evangelism and nurture known as the catechumenate. This will be discussed in the next chapter.

But I am sure it was also because of worship. On Sunday evenings we had a service of devotion to the Blessed Sacrament. This was largely a time of silence. Effort was made to create an atmosphere of stillness and an opportunity for reflection. The focus was the presence of Jesus in the Eucharistic bread, but by implication his presence in all creation.

Although this was not attended by great numbers it was very popular among young people. It was about the only service in the week when newcomers would regularly just turn up. It was possible just to wander in. There was no need to say anything. In a church culture where even singing a hymn implies shared belief in what the hymn is saying, these services provided a still focus for those who felt a spiritual yearning, but did not yet want the dialogue of enquiry, so much as the adoration of encounter, a sacred space to meet a living God. Worship of this sort, including special vigils of prayer, like a service for peace at the time of the Gulf crisis, whole days of silent prayer, special services of healing and reconciliation, raised the spiritual temperature of the church. As attendance at the daily Eucharist grew, and as people came to be changed by the grace and intimacy of these healing sacraments, the church started to become the house of prayer which is still what our spiritually thirsty world is longing for. Best of all, as the spiritual temperature rose to apostolic level, the spontaneous combustion of Christ-like witness and ordinary everyday evangelism began to happen. People shared their faith with their friends and invited them to church.

Further Questions
- How does your church serve the needs of your community? How can you find out what those needs are?
- How are the sacraments made available to all the people of your community and your church?
- Are there regular services of healing and reconciliation?
- Is the Eucharist clothed only in the culture of a previous age or is it being expressed in a fresh way for people of our day?

5

Travelling Before Arriving:
The Overlap Between Outreach and Nurture

Catholic evangelism is concerned with the journey of faith. Evangelism which begins in service, dialogue and relationship proceeds by way of an accompanied journey. This is the overlap between outreach and nurture. It is also the language of the catechumenate, a word that takes its root from catechesis, meaning instruction, but is actually more about transformation than information.

The catechumenate is a process whereby people are accompanied on a journey from interested unbelief, the point of contact between the committed faith of the church and the aspirant desires of the world, to active discipleship. It also recognizes that all of us are on this journey. Nobody is ever fully evangelized. In this way the sharing of faith is not simply the passing on of a tradition or a message but is the establishment of a relationship, the sharing of a journey. There are things to be learned, but the most important thing is to be in relationship with the guide. Through this relationship one discovers and appropriates the truth of Christian faith. It is a journey in the company of Jesus, but also in the company of the church. Enquirers are accompanied on the journey by members of the church; they are incorporated into the life of the church as well as being taught the Christian faith. The church itself becomes a pilgrim people.

Pilgrim Companions

Pilgrimage is a powerful metaphor, not only for the individual journey of a Christian soul, but for the whole understanding of the church and the gospel. We are on a journey home. We make this journey in the company of Jesus who has, like the good shepherd seeking the lost sheep, come down from heaven to meet us where we are and show us the way. We also make it in the company of other believers. We have made a decision to follow Christ and to live a new life. We are also committed to show others who are lost in the puzzle of human life the way through the maze.

This understanding has a liberating effect on evangelism. We do not need to persuade or cajole anybody into believing. Evangelism is an expression of love, flowing from worship and inspired by the self-giving of God in the Incarnation. The evangelistic task is expressed in service, relationship and journey. Along the way we will find ample opportunity to bear witness to the truth we have discovered. Evangelism will no longer be about finding the right words, but living the right life, heading in the right direction. The wrong choices people make will have to be powerfully challenged but this will arise from within a relationship that is marked by service and love, and will not intrude from outside. Sometimes evangelism seems arrogant—Jesus is the answer, now what was the question? When you begin to listen, when you begin to make yourself vulnerable to the needs of individuals, when you start accompanying them on their journey through life, even if this appears like compromise to others (and let us remind ourselves again that it was this seeming compromise which was the precise complaint the religiously orthodox made against Jesus) then the call of repentance is heard as the call of a loving Father, not wanting to chastise his children, but to enfold them in his love.

It is one of the achievements of the Decade of Evangelism that it has reminded the church of this vital link between evangelism and nurture. Very few people become Christians in an instant. John Finney's research shows a gradual unfolding of faith as the norm for most people.[1] Our evangelistic strategy must take note of this and develop ways of accompanying people on the road. The specific insights of the catechumenate provide an excellent model for all churches, but especially those of a catholic tradition since a great emphasis is put on the role of the worshipping community as a missionary congregation, and on incorporation into the church as a necessary part of becoming a Christian. However, there are other things we can learn from the pilgrimage metaphor.

Invitation to Journey

We need to find ways of meeting people where they are. Understanding the link between evangelism and service will be the key. But most churches, especially Anglican ones, have a huge number of contacts with people anyway. What we are bad at is making good use of them. We need to offer people something other than an invitation to church or a challenge to be converted. Steve Croft, in his excellent CPAS handbook, *Growing New Christians*, echoes from an evangelical tradition the findings of the catechumenate and talks about stepping stones towards the life of faith—places where the people we are in contact with can move towards the life of faith. Every church community needs to work hard at establishing neutral ground where those who are searching for some kind of deeper meaning to their lives can explore the claims of the Christian faith and, more importantly, *experience* and *receive* the love and service of Christian people and the grace of God.

We need to develop expertise in accompanying these people on their journey. We need good resources, but most of all we need to foster in people a desire to lead others to Christ. God will always be the Evangelist. But we are called to be midwives, cooperating in his mission, ensuring safe delivery of the new life.

We need a fresh spirituality, one that is filled with high expectations of what God can do. Catholics are so good at worshipping Christ in the sacraments and believe in God's transforming power, but are sometimes guilty of putting limits on God's sovereignty. There is a lock on the tabernacle. But he who is able to

---

1   John Finney, *Finding Faith Today* (Bible Society, 1992) p 24.

transform bread and wine into his body and blood can be enfleshed in all sorts of people and in many different places. We adore the presence of Jesus in a broken piece of bread in order to see him in the brokenness of the world.

People do not become Christians because they have been persuaded to believe. Apologetics has a vital role in the contemporary church, but in the end people become Christians because it makes sense of their life. It is a personal commitment. And God does not want people as slaves but as free lovers. One of the great Anglo-Catholic slum priests, Fr Basil Jellicoe, spoke of the people of God as 'blood brothers and sisters of the King of Kings.' This is the great scandal of the gospel: we are to be co-heirs with Christ, family members, not just friends. This demands the free response of love that is the true turning to Christ that the word 'repentance' describes. Our whole life is orientated towards him who orientated his whole life towards us.

Our freedom to choose marks our humanity. God created us out of free love, and has made us able to love freely. He shows us his love in such a way that our freedom to choose how we respond is safeguarded. Even at the Resurrection Jesus was not instantly recognized. And so often we reject his love. The fall of humanity is about our wrong choices, but our ability to choose remains. Evangelism is, therefore, always about invitation more than persuasion. It is about presenting choices. We are firm about what we believe, and the reasonableness and intellectual credibility of faith, but most of all we share our love.

The Journey of Nurture

It is when we realize that we are still on the journey ourselves, that even the sacraments are foretastes of a glory which still awaits us, and that we need to constantly re-orientate our lives to Christ, that we are able to act as midwives with the Evangelist God who alone brings people to relationship with him. We invite God to be at work in us, forming Christ in our hearts as he was formed in the womb of Mary.

The church which wishes to go on pilgrimage must, therefore, give special attention to the discipling of the people it already has so that everyone grows in their faith. There is a huge problem of stunted growth in many churches: people who have been attending worship for years, often very faithfully, but who do not really know God. Many catholic parishes have been particularly guilty at not nurturing people in the faith. Rather than complain at these people, or worse sit in judgment on them, we should develop programmes of discipleship. The point is that this will bear fruit in mission—not just more people active as Christians, but people radiant with the love of God, attracting people to the gospel even before they do or say anything.

We could also mention here the particular power of actually making a pilgrimage to a holy place. Because of our belief in the Incarnation we understand that there are particular people and places where God is powerfully present. He makes himself the somewhere God in the scandal of this particularity in order that he may be known everywhere. We honour these particular people as saints, and they are always powerful evangelists, because Jesus is seen so clearly in them. Think only of the magnetic charm of Mother Theresa of Calcutta or Brother Roger of Taizé. We need to visit these particular places because God has marked them out for us as reminders of his love of the material world and his desire to make his dwelling place with us. By making such a pilgrimage we are reminded that the whole of our life is a journey home.

Putting It Into Practice

Some churches, wanting to explore this way of approaching evangelism, have held one-off meetings on neutral ground, often a room in a pub, entitled something like 'Is life a four letter word?' as a way of gathering together people who are interested in finding out more about life (and by implication more about God). Someone speaks about life and faith, there is a way of stimulating discussion and questions, some thought-provoking entertainment and some food and drink. The results are surprising. Because the invitation is to come and see, and provided the next step is in place, many churches are discovering that people are happy to begin, be it ever so tentatively, a journey to faith. This bears out the widely held view that we live in an age of spiritual renewal, but not, as yet, an age when interest in spirituality leads people to the church. Change the way the church is perceived, and the way it does its evangelism and it is not hard to find people who are hungry to find out more and thirsty for an experience of God.

In my experience this sort of activity is always fruitful. Once we held a question time evening on social, moral and spiritual issues, and the gospel had to do battle with other secular philosophies and viewpoints. Many non-Christians attended. Contact was made, and for a few a journey was begun. Alongside this, great effort was made to establish the catechumenate and groups for faith-sharing and prayer so the whole people of God could grow in their discipleship.

Because the whole of life is a journey we also regularly went on pilgrimage. Every summer the young people of the parish walked hundreds of miles on pilgrimage to places such as Canterbury and Walsingham. Although undertaken for the renewal of faith, several teenagers found themselves turning to Christ along the road of pilgrimage. They had come for the challenge of walking a hundred miles; celebrating the Eucharist at the side of the road or in a tatty church hall with a tin cup chalice and a hunk of bread they met Jesus Emmanuel. Their conversion on the road became a metaphor and an encouragement for a pilgrim church.

Further Questions

- If you were to meet someone tonight and they said they would like to find out more of what life was really all about what could your church offer them?
- Are groups for enquirers and those further on in the journey a regular part of your church's life ?

6

Spirituality Before Doctrine:
The Overlap Between Outreach and Worship

The emphasis of catholic evangelism is that the Christian faith is a way of life and not just things to believe in. We have explored this at some length, but we now need to remind ourselves that the end of all our endeavour and our journeying is God. We love the church, we love the sacraments, we love the Scriptures, but we love them because they give us access to God. We love one another, but we are able to love because we are made in the image of God and because the love we have inside us is that image. We even love Jesus, not as an end in itself, but because he is the way to the Father.

Mission begins with worship and it ends in worship. It flows from God's revelation of himself in creation and redemption and it ends in recreation and in the enjoyment of God for ever. It is for this reason that the best word to describe the Christian life remains the first word that was used—the Way. There are many examples of the dynamic use of this word in the gospels and in the Acts of the Apostles. Jesus describes himself as 'the Way' (John 14.6) and the first disciples are known as followers of the Way (Acts 9.2) before they are known as Christians. The *Didache*, the earliest surviving Christian document outside the New Testament, picks up this theme describing the faith as the 'way of life' (*Didache* Part 1.1). This way of life is the way of relationship with God, the fullness of life Jesus promises to those who love him.

We have already spoken about the sacraments but it is important to emphasize here not only the converting power of worship but also the sustaining reality of prayer.

St Paul says, 'Always be joyful; pray constantly' (1 Thessalonians 5.17). I do not think he means do that activity we call prayer constantly. Nor does he mean go around with a fixed grin on your face all the time. But make your life a prayer and then you will find true joy. Seek to make every moment an offering of praise to God the Father. This is the way of holiness, which means wholeness, catholic. It is the focusing of our life in Christ and will bring the wholeness and the holiness we long for. This is the source of joy and the aim of prayer. Our hearts will always be restless until they find their rest in the sacred, broken and human heart of Jesus.

Not only will this require some regular discipline about times of prayer, though the way these times are used and the ways they are expressed will vary enormously from one person to the next, but also regular and wise spiritual counsel. This again is one of the distinctive gifts of catholic spirituality to the expression of evangelism. For many people a search for God will begin with a restlessness about life, a sense that all rhythm has gone out of life, a feeling of either enforced idleness or insufferable busyness. Our society is either frantic or idle, but there is very little stillness. The stillness of prayer, the sacred space of a place of prayer, a place set aside and carefully arranged and suitably adorned, is an enormous attraction. Brother Roger of Taizé said that 'when the church becomes a house of prayer the people will come running.' This will happen when people's lives are centred on God. Mission ceases to be an activity, often unwittingly mimicking the frantic busyness of the world and its obsession with results, and becomes an attitude. We are mission, rather than mission being something we do. And because we have planned our strategy the right way round, beginning with spirituality, what we do clearly arises out of what we are called to be. Evangelism must involve doing things, but it will begin and end in our being, our relationship with God, our prayer. Often the most evangelistically effective things we do will be the ordinary affairs of our life conducted differently and with an attitude of thanksgiving and love.

For catholic Christians the Eucharist will be right at the heart of this. If evangelism is linked to worship, and if it is about the giving and receiving of love, then the love feast of the church, the means by which we participate in the life of heaven, will be the constant source of strength, a bold and living testimony of all we proclaim and believe, and the place where, in this life, we bring our burdens and our joys. We will bring to the altar those who are searching for meaning in life and those who are thirsty for love. We will bring our disappointments, our rejections and our failings, knowing that Christ is with us at the point of this exchange between humanity and God making present the supreme sacrifice of Calvary.

The Eucharist will be understood not as the remembering of the past but the breaking in of the future. Our communion is with a Risen Lord and through him with the church everywhere both on earth and in heaven. This is the chief reason catholic Christians have a high doctrine of the communion of saints. Not just because they were good people, but because worship and mission go together. By their example the saints show us how to live the Christian life in a way that is powerfully attractive to the world as well as powerfully challenging to those who have put down their roots in the world. By their prayers they show us the end of all Christian endeavour is God and love of him alone. They show us the church as it really is, now seen in a glass darkly, but then face to face. With the saints we shall live with God for ever.

Putting It Into Practice

There is so much that could be said about the beautiful and grace-filled ways a church begins to grow, but always it is the work of God. If there is one lesson to learn it is to pray and to be faithful, to plough and sow before you even think of harvest. When I had been in the parish a short time and was feeling at a low ebb I prayed that God would send me some help. A few weeks later a couple turned up at the church. They had recently moved to the area. They were a huge support because they both prayed. The wife came to the Mass virtually every day and also to the Morning Office. She prayed every night for the church, and often used to come to the church before dawn to pray for the church and community. When I moved on I thanked her. I firmly believe that despite all the effort to get strategy and planning right, it could only be right if it was in communion with the heart of God, and it was her prayer, more than anything else, that had kept us there.

The building was always kept open, despite theft and vandalism and once an arson attack—which I interpreted as a sign that we must be doing something right! Once, the Paschal Candle was stolen. Someone said it had taken by an angel. I was not too sure about this, but the reason given has always stayed with me. It was to remind us that the light and grace of Christ must shine within. Then others will see it. And it is irresistible.

Further Questions
- How does it feel to worship at your church on a Sunday morning?
- How is your life an advertisement for the gospel?